T0132351

ADVENTURES WITH MORGAN AND LUKAS

The First Day of School

KAT ARRIAGA

AuthorHouse™
1663 Liberty Drive
Bloomington, IN 47403
www.authorhouse.com
Phone: 1 (800) 839-8640

Published by AuthorHouse 08/15/2019

ISBN: 978-1-7283-1824-0 (sc)
ISBN: 978-1-7283-1823-3 (e)

Library of Congress Control Number: 2019908973

Print information available on the last page.

authorHOUSE®

To Morgan and Lukas, who taught me that every day is an adventure.

And to my husband, Kalani, who's unwavering love and support makes everything possible.

– L.U.G.

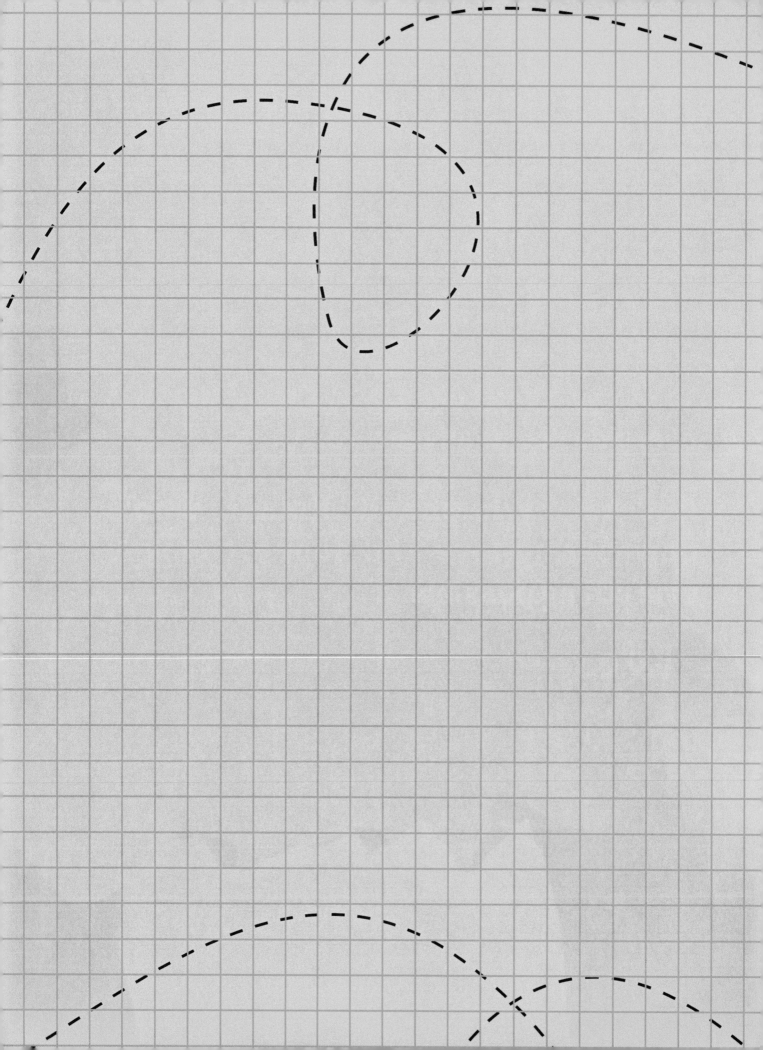

Today is Morgan and Lukas' first day of school.

Morgan is still in bed sleeping. She loves to sleep! When her body is ready and rested, she will slowly begin to open her eyes.

Lukas is already awake and eating breakfast. He is usually the first to get out of bed.

Mommy made Lukas his favorite things to eat- eggs, rice and tomatoes. Mommy also loves to eat rice, eggs and tomatoes.

The tomatoes are red and juicy. Mommy grinds a little bit of pink Himalayan sea salt over the cut up tomatoes to bring out the flavor.

What's your favorite thing to eat for breakfast?

Lukas hears footsteps coming down the stairs.

It's Morgan!

Mommy makes Morgan a sunny-side up egg with no tomatoes. Morgan doesn't like to eat many things. She is very picky. But she sure loves eggs, especially the yolk.

Who's the pickiest eater in your family?

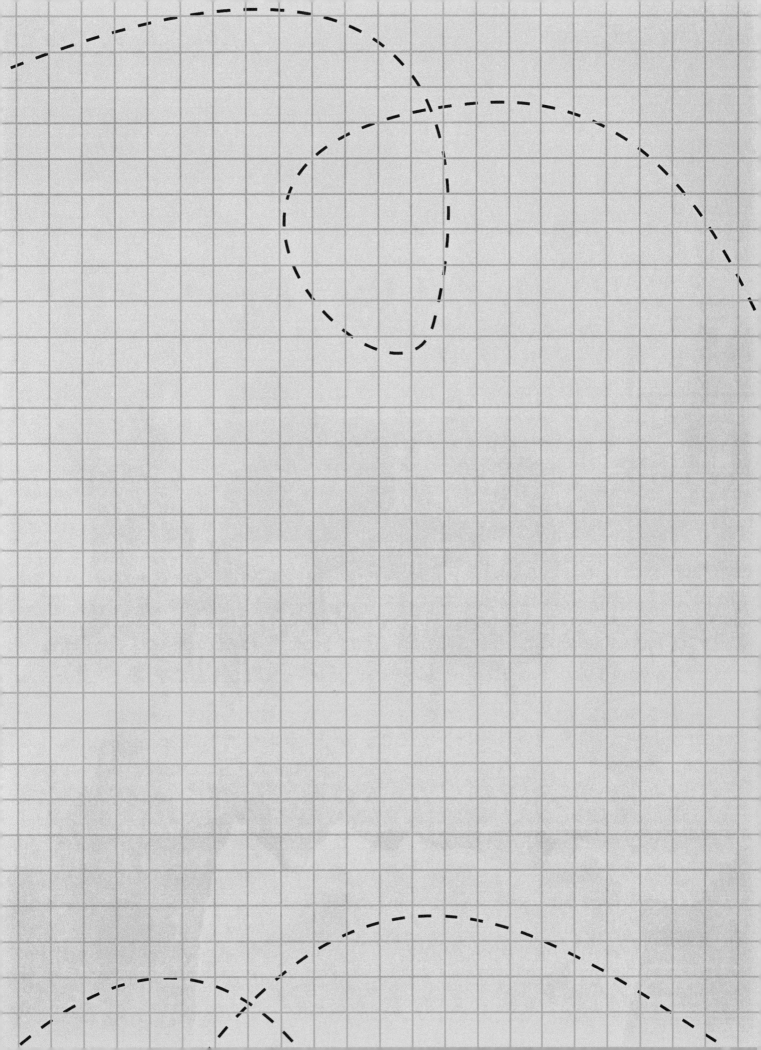

After breakfast, Morgan and Lukas are ready to play. They head upstairs to the loft where their toys are.

In the middle of the room is a large square table with four chairs. This is where they sometimes do their schoolwork.

Morgan goes straight to the train table where she likes to play with her building bricks.

Lukas picks a sticker book off the shelf and brings it to the table to work on. He loves playing with sticker books.

The sticker book is all about cavemen. Lukas has fun putting together mammoth hunting scenes and decorating the caves.

Morgan sees what her brother is working on and wants to join too! She goes over to the shelf and picks out her own sticker book.

Morgan picks the book about vacations. She enjoys creating scenes from different parts of the world.

Lukas notices something strange in the room.

"Hey, where'd that come from?"

"That wasn't there yesterday," Morgan says.

Mommy takes a look.

"That's a microscope."

A microscope is a tool that lets you see things that are very, very small.

Mommy shows Morgan and Lukas how to use the microscope.

Morgan and Lukas take turns looking at the slides. Microscope slides are very thin pieces of glass that hold things.

The slides are red, yellow and blue.

The red slides have insects. Morgan and Lukas take turns looking at a locust leg, a honeybee antenna and dragonfly wings. The dragonfly wings are Morgan's favorite.

The yellow slides have plants. Morgan and Lukas take turns looking at bamboo, flower pollen and onion skin. The onion skin looks like a stack of bricks!

The blue slides have animals. Morgan and Lukas take turns looking at bird feathers, rabbit hair and goldfish scales. Lukas likes looking at the goldfish scales.

Mommy gets 2 pieces of blank paper and brings it over to the table. One piece of paper is for Morgan and one piece of paper is for Lukas.

Mommy gives each of them a pencil to write with and asks them to write their names as best as they can.

"I need help, Mommy," Lukas says.

Mommy comes over to Lukas to help him. He is still learning how to write his letters.

Mommy goes to the other room to gather materials for the next activity. She comes back bringing a box of crayons, a box of markers and some painting supplies.

She asks Morgan and Lukas to each pick out which art medium they would like to use.

Morgan loves to draw with markers. She likes the bright bold colors and the markers are easy to hold. She takes a purple marker and draws a beautiful dragonfly. She adds pink and yellow to its wings.

Do you have a favorite color?
What is it?

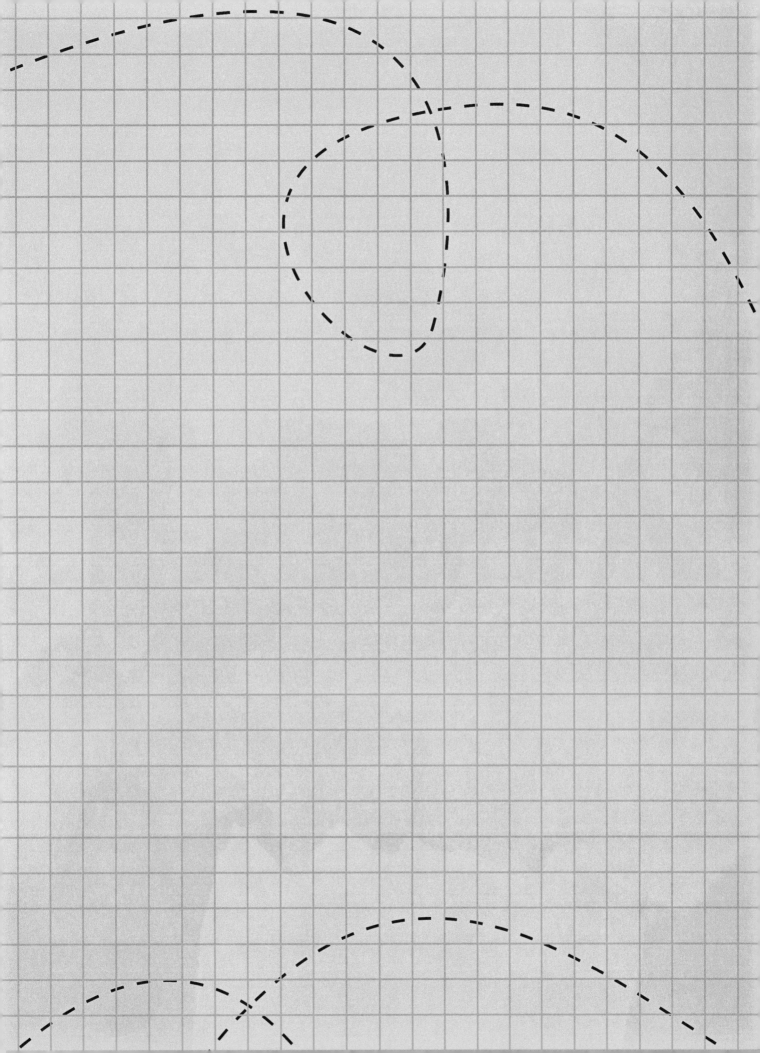

Lukas loves to paint. Mommy gets a palette ready for him.

"What colors would you like?"

Lukas chooses orange, blue and yellow.

Mommy carefully squeezes the tubes of paint and fills Lukas' palette.

Next, Mommy helps him set up the easel. An easel helps to hold the paper while Lukas paints.

Lukas paints a colorful goldfish!

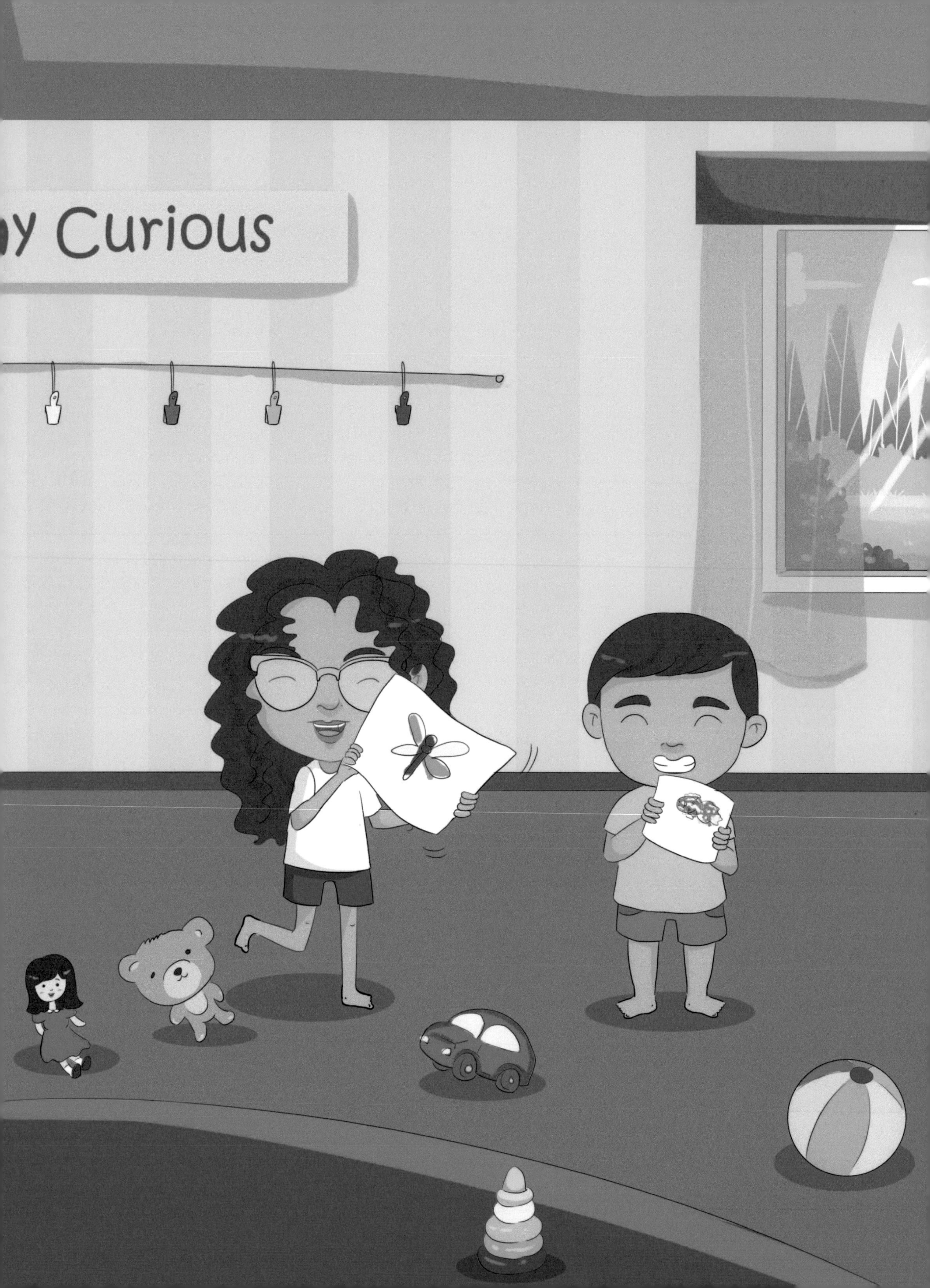
y Curious

Morgan and Lukas enjoy making art.

Lukas holds up his goldfish.

"Look! My goldfish is swimming!"

Morgan holds her dragonfly up as high as she can.

"Oh yeah? My dragonfly is flying!!!"

"Alright you two, it's time to clean up!"

Lukas takes the microscope slides and sorts them by color. He counts each slide as he puts them back in the box. There's 30!

What number can you count up to?

Morgan helps collect all of the markers and neatly puts them back in the box. But, first, she makes a tower of markers by stacking them on top of each other. She likes to see how many she can stack before it starts to lean and topple over.

Mommy takes the palette and paint brushes and cleans them off in the sink. It's pretty when the paint runs off in the water.

It's a wavy rainbow!

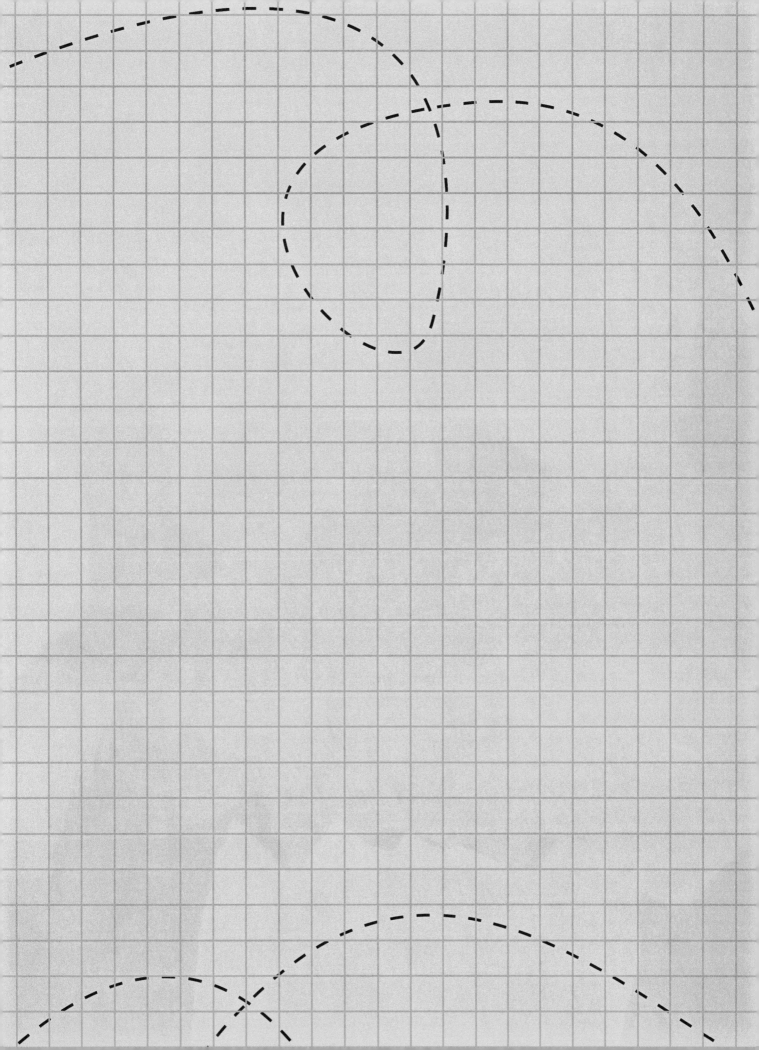

Morgan and Lukas are excited to hang their artwork on the wall.

The cable where they display their artwork is too high for them to reach.

They take chairs from the table so they can stand on them to reach the cable.

Morgan drags her chair back to the table.

"I can't wait to show Daddy!"

"Me too!" Lukas says.

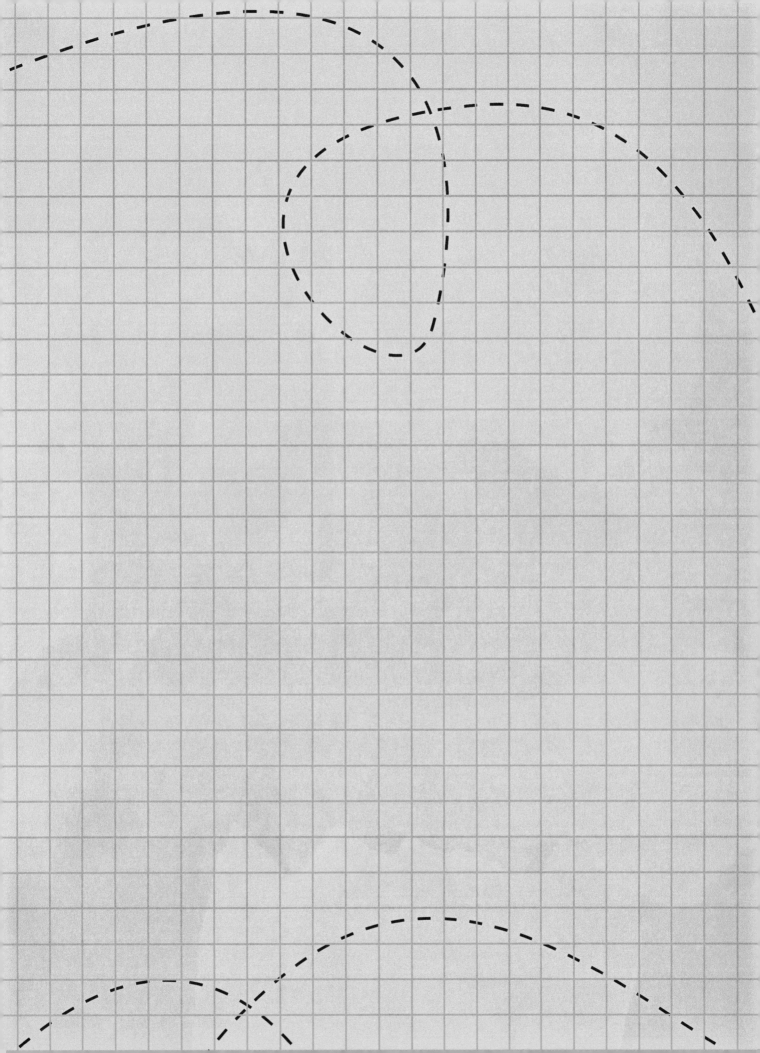

It was a good first day of school.

About The Book

Morgan and Lukas find something strange in their playroom. What could it be? Follow along as they learn through play on the first day of school!

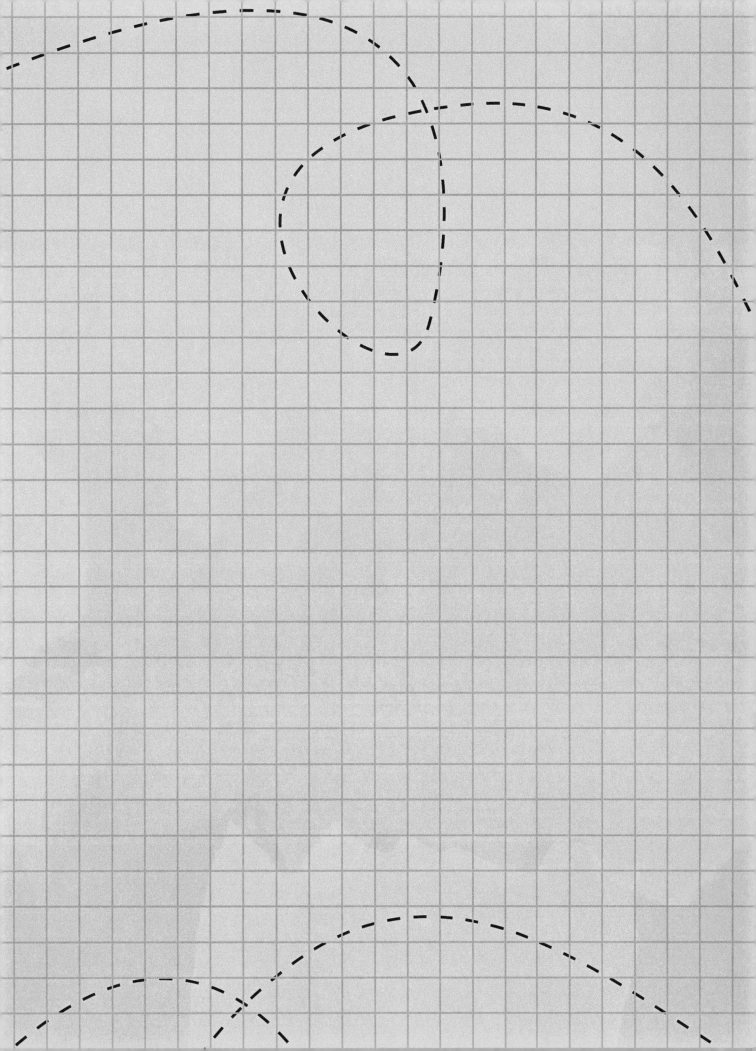

Printed in the United States
By Bookmasters